The
RELUCTANT
LE▲DER

Craig S. Galati

THE RELUCTANT LEADER

iUniverse books may be ordered through booksellers or by contacting:

iUniverse
1663 Liberty Drive
Bloomington, IN 47403
www.iuniverse.com
844-349-9409

ISBN: 978-1-6632-2943-4 (sc)
ISBN: 978-1-6632-2963-2 (e)

Library of Congress Control Number: 2021920176

Print information available on the last page.

iUniverse rev. date: 10/04/2021

Dedication

To Sally, Corin, and Carson

CONTENTS

CONTENTS

ACKNOWLEDGMENTS

Many thanks!

Alex Raffi and Brian Rouff of Imagine Communications for cover design, book editing, and overall encouragement.

The staff of LGA Architecture, especially for their continual support.

John Haddad for being the best business partner anyone could have.

Jason Jorjorian and Lance Kirk — the next generation is yours.

Arvind Menon, Brad Tope, Donna Meyer, and Patrick Sullivan of Meadows Bank.

Randy Garcia and Michelle Konstantarakis of Investment Counsel Company.

Lora Hendrickson

Enrique Villar and Abdullah Alotaibi of Radioactive Productions.

Gary Krape, CPA

In memory of Julie Pagliaro.

FOREWORD

Leadership is the breath—the oxygen—that animates successful enterprises. At their best, breath and leadership are subtle if not invisible, but we know they enliven people and organizations. We also notice when the breath of leadership in organizations is halting or erratic. In such situations, we come to understand leadership in terms of what it is not, by what is missing, as reflected in the inspiration-deprived mistakes we make or witness, or by the essential decisions we defer, and/or by the messages we send that deflate and misdirect when we want to inspire and guide.

In some ways, leadership is like coaching kids' sports: the coach as the leader must be positive and inspire, support, influence, and persuade by word and personal example. There is little value or benefit in kids' sports or business for the directive command, except in those rare moments when morale is high and the need for decisiveness and action is urgent. And fortunately, modern leaders have a choice of several effective leadership styles. But when the leader, as coach, misreads the type of leadership style a situation most needs, feedback is usually quick and clear—poor execution, passive-aggressive behavior, overt resistance, or rejection—or even failure.

Such are the lessons of leadership Craig Galati knows well, with over ten years of experience resurrecting an enterprise under the most daunting of circumstances, including his own uncertainty about whether he was up to the job—hence his being "the Reluctant Leader."

Craig learned to lead by being thrust into an organizational cauldron brewing with potentially toxic elements, each of which could kill any lesser organization: national economic recession; large financial debt, including personal and onerous guarantees; a departing charismatic partner; another dysfunctional non-team oriented partner; a shrunken market for its services; a very sick key team member; a confused organizational identity; and bankers who, well, were fulfilling their profession's worst stereotype.

And yet Craig, his key partner, John, and the firm survived, evolved, and eventually thrived—a leadership success story. That story is told here, with stark honesty, self awareness, and lessons learned—all acquired by Craig from his firm's challenging experiences.

Craig and I have been friends for more than two decades. Over that time, I have sometimes been a mentor or a coach, but most of the time I have been a privileged witness to his leadership journey. I have seen his growth and transformation as he came to understand what matters to him, as he became aware of and took modest pride in his own unique leadership talents, and to see him continuously learn from the resulting successful transformation of his firm.

In these pages, you'll read how Craig's architecture firm, LGA, has grown as a purpose-driven organization, focused on service and the creation of unique experiences, drawing on a wellspring of professional and human values like integrity, excellence, empathy, and generosity, and most importantly, placing their clients' and their community's interests above their own.

The results are trusting relationships with clients, staff, consultants, and community stakeholders. Key to that trust is transparency, honesty, and vulnerability; thinking, speaking and acting what is true whether it accords with popular opinion or not, because that is what it means, Craig writes, to be a professional.

This book is the story of Craig's pilgrimage toward the goal of effective leadership. As such, it is an intriguing story about a unique man and his firm. But the most important reason for you to read this book is to help you weather the inevitable storms of business and of life, taking inspiration and courage from his example, and then to dream your own leadership path and enjoy that invigorating breath of wisdom in your own personal and organizational life.

Lou Marines
Consultant, Founder of Advanced Management Institute (AMI), author of *The Language of Leadership*

PROLOGUE

Though the sun was shining, it was a cold winter day by Las Vegas standards. There were hints of snow on the distant mountains. Much of the country was in the midst of the Great Recession, which started sometime in the middle of 2007. Business had slowed and many companies had laid off and furloughed employees at a rate not seen before in Las Vegas. Southern Nevada's reliance on gaming, tourism, and housing sales had proven to be futile, bringing its booming economy to its knees. In all the years I have lived here, I have never seen the community hit by a recession, especially one of this magnitude.

On this cold day, I found myself standing at the edge of my parents' gravesite in Boulder City, Nevada, a short drive from downtown Las Vegas, at eleven in the morning. Not that the time mattered.

I didn't remember driving to the cemetery, but there I was, anxious, and wondering what I was doing there. I last remembered walking into the office early in the morning.

It was December 22, 2011.

I remember thinking it was just a few days away from Christmas.

A rush of emotions came over me—fear, anxiety, dread. I was a fifty-one-year-old man running home to his parents for advice and counsel. I was in crisis. My firm was over $800,000 in debt, our founding partner had just resigned, and we had very little work—certainly not enough to sustain the rent and the few employees who were left. I had no idea where to turn, what to do, or how we were going to pull through this. My heart ached unlike anything I had ever felt before.

Earlier in the week, I met with my two remaining partners to discuss the situation. During the meeting, it was agreed that with the resignation of our founder, I would take over the leadership of the company. Although I agreed to take this role, I had very little idea of what it really meant or what it would entail. Even though I had never managed or led the company, especially in difficult times, I did realize it would be a difficult road ahead. The path looked daunting.

The drive from Boulder City to Las Vegas is delightful, through a mountain pass that traverses the southern edge of Henderson, Nevada. The mountains are beautiful and offers a view of the entire Las Vegas valley. I drove back with a renewed sense of purpose, as if my parents' wisdom had been transferred to me. I knew what I had to do. I needed to save this company, save the few jobs left, and be steadfast in giving this problem my all—or die trying. Once back in the office, my business partner, John, and I agreed we would bring the company back; it seemed the easier path was bankruptcy but neither of us wanted that. Little did we know the work that was ahead of us.

Background

Most of us remember the Great Recession. Although as a firm we were aware of it from the beginning, we just didn't pay attention to the warning signs. As it turned out, it was the most difficult time in our firm's history. It whittled away at our workload, cash flow, and ability to keep our staff employed until by October of 2011, we had spent all of our savings, laid off most of our staff, and cut our expenses to the bone.

Early on we were insulated from the true effects of the recession as we had a few large federal contracts, but as those ended, we had very little in the pipeline and reacted too slowly. The beginning of the end really happened to us from July to October 2011 where we used all of our cash reserves to keep our staff employed, even though there was very little work to do, hoping that the next big contract was right around the corner. But by November of 2011, cash reserves were gone, staff was reduced as much as we could—everyone who remained was given a 50% salary cut and the partners were not taking a paycheck—and there was the debt, $840,000.

The worst thing about our debt was that over $600,000 was owed to our consultants for work they had completed in good faith and had benefitted our clients. Work that we invoiced and collected, but we did not pay out. It still sickens me to think we were capable of doing this, but once on the slippery slope, the slide picks up speed until it is insurmountable. We could no longer rob from Peter to pay Paul.

Enter leadership. I had never really wanted to be the firm leader. While I led the business development efforts of the firm, I was not heavily involved in the other areas of firm leadership and management such as cash flow planning, staff allocation, and overall planning for the future to the extent that I thought I could competently lead. These would be critical elements for me to learn to chart our way back from the depths of financial ruin.

Morale was low, resources were non-existent, and we didn't have the cash to pay our rent or bills. My leadership timing was impeccable!

I really was The Reluctant Leader.

What I did have: a strong family, a supportive network, a desire to turn the company around, a great business partner, and a committed staff. These would be the critical components for recovery. I couldn't really ask for much more!

The following story highlights the lessons learned throughout this crisis in hopes that those who read this can take advantage of them to accelerate their growth curve and be more prepared for a role in leadership. It is never too early to prepare yourself … for one day, leadership may choose you.

LESSON ONE

IT TAKES GRIT TO SURVIVE!

LESSON ONE

It Takes Grit to Survive!

Grit is an interesting word, one I never thought of using prior to 2011. But it is the most appropriate word I can think of to describe what was necessary during a time of crisis. Angela Duckworth, a psychology professor at the University of Pennsylvania, coined the term grit and defines it as:

"The quality of being able to sustain your passions, and also work really hard at them, over really disappointingly long periods of time."

My parents were strong, value-based people who worked very hard for their family. I remember my dad saying to me once, "Never get out-worked by anyone; it's the only thing you can control." My parents taught my brothers and me to never steal and to always pay our debts. I could not believe the firm accumulated the magnitude of debt that it did. My business partner and I vowed that we would make it right, even though we weren't sure how. Paying off our debts became a strong driver of our mindset and focused our attention. Our values screamed at us to make it right. We also enacted several things to accomplish this goal and to keep it from happening again. I'll touch on those in another chapter.

I was embarrassed, guilt ridden, and feeling very inauthentic, all things I loathed. But I knew the only path was to work hard. This chapter highlights some of our immediate actions.

Hit the Issues Head On

When we set our course, albeit fluidly, to overcome our debt, create a strong company, and still be standing to take care of our clients as the economy recovered, we knew we needed to hit the issues head on. The first thing I did was call all our creditors personally. This act may have been the single most important thing we did as it let our creditors know we were aware of and working on formulating a plan. I respectfully asked for time to get my arms around the situation, which most of our creditors allowed. Hiding behind the issues or dodging calls was not an authentic way forward. Many of the people we owed told me they were owed money from other organizations but that we were the first ones to call and acknowledge the problem. This act of good faith carried us forward and helped us buy the precious time we needed to address the issues.

To solve our problems, the most important thing we needed was new revenue. The firm had been awarded two projects six months earlier; one was caught up in federal politics, and the other was moving slowly because of the municipality being shorthanded. We couldn't do much regarding the federal project as we needed to wait for Congress to enact a new provision in the Southern Nevada Public Lands Management Act, which was the total source of funding for the project. Congress seemed to be in no hurry then (as if they ever are), as they hadn't even funded the government for the year. While these two projects were not enough to sustain the firm, they certainly would provide some breathing room and allow us to begin to plan our repayment of debt. Starting these projects would give us the shot in the arm that we really needed.

The municipal project was something we thought we could positively affect. I called the client's project manager and pleaded with him to get the project started. I offered to help him write the contract and assist him with any other paperwork he needed to get the project initiated and approved. I was fortunate that I had known him for some time and even though it was unorthodox, he allowed me to help and by February of 2012, we were officially awarded the project.

The federal project was finally funded and we were authorized to begin the work in March of 2012. We were a mere three months from our abrupt leadership transition and were starting to actually see a potential path forward. It was difficult for all of us as we still were not receiving full salaries (partners had not received a salary since November of the previous year) and these salary reductions were hard to explain at home. Although I had much discussion with my wife about the problem, I tried to hide it from my children as I didn't want them to worry. I know our staff was in a similar position. The stress from our office had infiltrated our homes.

I had been calling every creditor weekly since the beginning of January and now was the time to develop a plan and hope they would agree with it. There were two strategies: a secured creditor strategy (bank) and a non-secured strategy (consultants) with each needing unique attention and focus.

Secured Strategy. While the bank line of credit was certainly a concern because our former founding partner and I were personal guarantors on approximately $140,000, the actual line of credit did not come up for renewal until May, so we decided to continue to make the interest payments on time and deal with our other creditors first. I knew that as long as we were paying interest, we could buy time.

Non-Secured Strategy. Dealing with the consultant debt was much harder to address. There were over thirty different consultants who were owed money, with some preparing to work on our new projects. Three had large balances, encompassing over half of the debt. This is where we started. I negotiated two-year notes, asking that they allow us to begin payments in May. To my amazement, they all agreed, although one very reluctantly. (I'll tell that story later.) The willingness to work with us gave me great faith in humans and fed our drive to pay them all back.

We decided there were a few smaller consultants we could just pay out in a few payments and clear off the books. The others were going to need to be a part of a loan strategy that I hoped I could work out with the bank in the next few months, or perhaps we could pay a little here and there as we brought in additional cash. I explained that we could make a small payment against what we owed and the plan was to get a loan by early summer and put this behind us.

We were buying time and that is what we needed.

Leadership is Situational

There are many styles of leadership and thousands of books written on the subject. Each of us has a default style, or a style of leadership in which we are most comfortable. Mine is a supportive or coaching style. It falls in line with Servant Leadership, which I believe in very much.

Dr. Paul Hershey wrote *The Situational Leader* in 1984. Little did I know that this book would be so important to me in early 2012. In case you haven't read the book, I suggest you do as it puts so many things in perspective with regard to leadership and one's ability to adapt to various situations.

Hershey describes leadership style as: "The patterns of behavior (words or actions) of the leader as perceived by others."

I never thought that one might actually plan the style of leadership to be used in different situations, but I am convinced that adapting my style situationally during this time of crisis was a key to our firm's success. I noticed a need for adaptation in my first meeting with our staff. None of them had been through a situation like this and they looked to me for answers. I remember the piercing eyes looking for reassurance and answers. I thought, *I don't have the answers*, and wondered how they perceived me as a leader.

I sensed that we were all in crisis albeit with differing emotions and risks, but my staff needed me to take a more directive approach and help them see the path forward and how they could be part of the recovery. We did not have time for consensus decision-making; staff were looking to be told what to do and when it needed to be accomplished. I shared the problems with staff and told them that John and I would work on a plan and that their role would be to take care of our clients and to treat them like gold (which they were and still are doing today). I decided to lead in a very transparent fashion, reporting each week on the progress of the firm and how we were getting through things.

As things progressed with the firm, I studied even more intently and worked on other leadership styles. I have identified six styles that I have tried to learn and practice where appropriate:

Visionary. This style is most appropriate when an organization needs a new direction. Its goal is to move people toward a new set of dreams or aspirations. I've found that the best visionary leaders help articulate where a group is going, but do not set the path or how best it should get there. This allows people to be free to innovate, experiment, and take risks. A visionary leader needs to be careful not to rethink the direction too often, which could lead to confusion in the organization.

Coaching. This style is best in one-on-one settings and focuses on developing individuals' skills and helping them connect their goals to those of the organization. Coaching works best with those individuals who show initiative and are open to coaching. A downside of this style is over-coaching where the leadership style begins to be perceived as micro-managing. Be careful.

Supportive. This style emphasizes teamwork and harmony in a group. The style is important when one is trying to heighten team chemistry, increase morale, improve communication, or repair broken trust. However, using this style in group settings too much can lead to the perception of the tolerance of poor performance and acceptance of mediocrity.

Democratic. The democratic style of leadership is focused on obtaining group commitment or consensus on goals. It works best when an organization has a strong vision as it allows pause to engage people's knowledge and skill in setting the direction for achieving the vision. It allows a leader to tap into the collective wisdom of the group. As the pace of this style of leadership is intentionally slow and relaxed, it can be devastating to an organization during a time of crisis or a need for quick decisions.

Pacesetting. This style demands a high standard for performance with the leader wanting the group to work better and faster. This style works well on a specific project where high performance and speed are essential to the project's success, but can be detrimental over time if used too often. It can lead to low morale and burn out.

Commanding. This classic military style of leadership works well in crisis where urgency is paramount. Used too often, this style becomes very ineffective as it limits room for relationship building and connections to people. But when a crisis is imminent and there is not time for debate, it is very effective.

A few things became clear to me as I was studying these styles and learning how to lead an organization of highly motivated professionals. The more you focus on improving yourself, the better leader you can become. Self-reflection and getting to know who you are, what values you hold, and where you want to go, form the paths you choose. While studying leadership styles will help you in different situations, the importance of building relationships with those around you is still a key to success. Those around you may have answers, but often they do not see the big picture. The more you can share and keep people in the loop the better their input can be used to help the organization.

At this moment I realized that leadership really is a team sport, but I have another chapter to talk about this important lesson.

Schedule is King

When an organization has tight cash flow and especially when you are paying debt, regular invoicing and collections become even more important. As we began to pick up new work, one of the most critical things we did was instill a mindset and ethic of starting and finishing on time. Design professionals have always struggled with meeting deadlines and this struggle had become the norm for our firm. Not that we disregarded schedules; to the contrary, we were better than most, but we still allowed delays of one to two weeks as acceptable. There is something cultural in our profession about the design never being complete. It's something I think we are all taught in school—we work until the last possible moment to finish and fall on the sword of design. This had to change in 2012.

We stressed to our staff the importance of meeting or even exceeding our obligations as a part of the path forward for the company. Without access to capital or a line of credit, we did not have the ability to bridge payroll and expenses—we could only rely on collections.

Operations were pulled a little closer to the vest and we met every week to review project schedules as well as cash in bank and collection status. While our firm had a good forecasting tool, we developed a new tool to understand our cash flow each week. Every Saturday, John and I would meet for a couple of hours and hand write the weekly cash flow plan on a yellow pad. We considered every expense and determined what we could pay this week and which ones we could pay the next. This meticulous study of every available dollar allowed us to make ends meet. Eventually the process became automated, but we still speak fondly of the "yellow spreadsheet." The more you immerse yourself into the business, the better decisions you can make. Once I did, the conversations with our bank and accountant greatly improved. These professions have their own language and learning it pays dividends.

When we negotiated the long-term notes with our consultants, one of the promises we made was to make sure that while we were paying the debt on the note, we would stay current on the new projects. This made it even more important to stay on schedule as we could not afford to fall behind, especially as we were digging out of our self-inflicted mountain of debt. But dig we did, a little at a time.

Staying on schedule is not always contingent on the design professional. The client and our consultant partners also play a part in the timely sequencing of work. It was a delicate balance with our clients as we could not let them know that we were cash poor. We had to anticipate any client delays and find a way around them. As I look back upon these times, I am still amazed at how smooth the projects went once we became more diligent about meeting the schedules. Throughout this crisis, we learned valuable skills that have stayed with us. We enacted a new policy to pay our consultant partners within ten days of being paid, instead of our previous agreement of thirty days. Our consultant partners appreciated this policy change and I believe worked even harder for us and our clients. Other new processes were established as follows:

Regular Check-ins. We initiated focused and regular check-ins with the project team, consultants, and the client. Depending upon the scale of the project and the duration of the schedule, the teams met weekly or biweekly to review progress, identify challenges, and solve problems. This practice has made us a better firm overall. It was borne out of a need, but continues to define our practice every day.

Anticipation. One of the gifts of 2012 was our staff learning how to anticipate issues and potential problems on our projects before they happened. I'm not sure how they developed this skill, but perhaps by staying so close to projects and not being spread thin on multiple jobs gave them this opportunity. During our weekly staff meetings, our project managers were able to give us a heads-up on project issues that helped us in managing the company and our cash flow.

Proactivity. Another process that was honed during this critical time was being proactive on staffing projects and understanding the effective utilization of resources. Prior to the 2011 crisis, it seemed that we were not very proactive with staffing projects appropriately, clearly understanding staff abilities and commitments, and meeting our deadlines every time. Sure, we did some great work in our early years, including the Springs Preserve, but that project cost the firm upwards of $1 million in time to complete successfully. Our new proactive approach has resulted in projects completed well, on time, and profitably, something we could not always boast about prior to 2011.

It is a testament to the group who was here then. Without these superstars, we could not have dug out of the hole we were in.

All In or Out

One thing I can tell you unequivocally is that tough times can galvanize an organization or rip it apart. Both happened to us. A core group of us became tighter, exposing the people who were not committed. It was important that the core group not tolerate the few who were not all in. An important lesson learned is that those who are not all in need to be encouraged to move on.

First a little context:

In 2011, our founding partner resigned and left the company, not because he didn't believe in our vision, but because he didn't think we would make it and didn't want to be on the hook for the debt. That was clear to me from the beginning and is even more clear today. Both he and I were signatory to the firm's line of credit and were personally liable for the balance owed on the line. At the beginning of 2012, that balance was $140,000. During our negotiations for his stock transfer, the only thing he really wanted was not to be held liable for this guarantee. I completely understood and most likely would not have wanted to be personally liable for a debt of a company I was leaving. We agreed that the company would stand in front of him on the debt if he would return his shares of stock and sign the separation agreement, but he would not do so until we removed him from the actual line of credit. This proved to be difficult since the bank would not give up this guarantee until we paid off the note, which we did not have the ability to do.

Banking is an interesting institution. I have many friends who are bankers and they are intelligent, caring, and all around good people. But many banks, including the bank we were with, are pretty black-and-white and formula driven. I won't even pretend to understand their business, but it has been my experience throughout my career that when you don't need a loan, the numbers justify your ability to receive one, and when you really need access to capital, they most likely don't. That was the position we found ourselves in early spring of 2012. We needed access to capital to pay off our consultant debt and we needed to refinance our line of credit balance to a longer term note.

I thought it would be easy: we borrow $300,000 over five years, pay off the existing line of credit, use $150,000 to pay off lingering debt, continue to pay off our consultant notes, and put the rest away as a rainy day fund. Simple, right?

The Call

Have you ever been excited to make a call because you knew you had a good plan and were going to be able to resolve an issue that had been bothering you? That's how I felt the day I called the bank. I had spent time preparing for the call and rehearsed questions I thought they would ask. I came into the office with a spirit of optimism. That day was going to be a good day and we would start the path to full recovery.

I prepared myself, took a deep breath, and made the call. I was able to speak with our loan officer and explained the situation—that we were coming out of difficult times, that we believed we could make payments that would support a new loan, that our founding partner was no longer with the firm, and that I would like to have him removed from the guarantee. After a long silence, the loan officer said he would look into the situation. He informed me that my former partner had already contacted him.

"Look, Craig, I'll tell you what I told him—we are not keen on giving away our guarantees until we are paid off; that is the purpose of them," the banker told me.

I told him that we would love to pay off the line, but we did not have access to that capital and would need to refinance over a longer term. He told me he would think about the situation and get back to me.

The anxiety hit again. It seemed that almost every week since November 2011, I had at least one anxiety attack—you know, the one with the hot flashes, the feeling of uncertainty, and confusion. But this one was different. I realized my simple plan wasn't going to be that simple. Being the eternal optimist, I knew I needed to wait to hear from the bank and hope for some good news. I couldn't dwell on the glass half empty.

It didn't take long for the banker to call me back. I knew this wasn't going my way when he asked if I had any other assets, cars, second properties, or 401k plans that I could draw from to satisfy the debt. The bank was unwilling to develop a longer term loan; the best they could offer was to pay it off in two payments one month apart. I thanked him and hung up. There was no way that was going to work. I began to think of ways to find additional capital, but was in a conundrum. I could not stop or defer any payments to the consultants I had agreed to pay, I had no access to additional capital, and even if I sold all my assets, there would not be enough to go around.

Visiting an Attorney

After looking at our finances and seeking many different options, my partner John and I decided we might need to reconsider the bankruptcy option. When you are in crisis, I guess it is good to look at every avenue to correct the problem, though I now realize there is never a silver bullet.

The attorney we visited was an old friend whose office was next door to our first office and John's wife had worked there previously, so it was easy to get an appointment. I had flashbacks of walking into the old office building. Our former suite was just across the hall from the attorney. We moved out in 1996 into a new and modern space, but the memories of a simpler time came flooding back to me. I remember the day that I first came to the office to discuss coming over to join the small firm of five people. I remember the mauve carpeting and I remember helping grow the firm to twenty people and needing to move to a larger space. Those times were some of the happiest memories of being in business. Perhaps not being the leader gave me that blissful life.

The attorney's office was just as I remembered it, like stepping back into the mid 1980s, the furniture and carpeting old and worn. The attorney greeted us with a smile and an offer to help. He specialized in bankruptcy and debt consolidation. He had been in practice for a very long time and we knew he would give us sage advice and not try to sell us on something we didn't want to do.

It's very hard to explain an embarrassing situation to someone. John and I didn't like to talk about it, and we were both extremely uncomfortable. But we knew that just like dealing with an addiction, the more we talked about it and took action, the better we would feel, though that still didn't make it enjoyable to admit our mistakes to another person who was not part of our inner circle. It made us feel inadequate regarding our business skills, which I guess we were. But, that too was changing!

After discussing our situation with him for thirty minutes, he said we were doing everything that a Chapter 11 reorganization would require us to do, but we seemed to be in control and didn't need to have a receiver manage our company for us. His recommendation was not to file for bankruptcy, but stay steadfast and perhaps contact another bank. We appreciated his guidance, as we really did not want a bankruptcy on our credit reports.

Maybe our business skills were better than we thought.

The New Bank

Years prior, we had designed several banks for Nevada First Bank. While we never did other business with them, they seemed to be well run and organized. They eventually sold to another bank and their president left to form a new community bank, Meadows Bank. We gave the president a call and he actually answered the phone. How refreshing! We set up a meeting with him to discuss our issues, how the bank might fit into our future plans, and how they could help now.

Meadows Bank was in a great position with an excellent board of directors. Since they were new in the market, they did not have the same bad loans that were eating away at the banking industry during the recession. And since they were a business bank, they avoided the foreclosures prevalent in the housing industry at that time.

Our meeting with the president went well, but there was a caveat. Since we were a new client, they would not be able to help us with enough money to buy out the previous bank, but they offered to coach us through a negotiation that we could afford. They requested that we move all of our business to the bank once we got through this and offered us an additional $50,000 line of credit to help make sure we could keep paying on the notes that we had and not worry about cashflow disruptions. I will never forget the president telling me, "We want to be your partner, not just your bank." That is how they treated us!

I will elaborate on this relationship and its impact in another chapter.

A Negotiated Deal

Over the summer of 2012, we had several negotiations with the bank that held our $140,000 line of credit on the terms of payout. Each scenario that the bank presented was better, but none met what we could do. However, we continued paying interest on the line, which is why I believe that the bank did not call the guarantees even though the note was overdue. Those negotiations with the bank were excruciating and at times lasted hours. It was exhausting. For some reason, each time we met with our loan officer, we needed to explain the situation again to him, like he had never heard of the problem. In the meantime, our former founding partner was also putting pressure on both our firm and the bank to resolve the issue.

In September of 2012, our loan officer called to set up a meeting with me and a couple of individuals from the bank. *Finally*, I thought, we were getting somewhere. I invited both of my partners to attend the meeting and was hopeful that we would get this issue resolved.

The meeting was set for a Thursday late afternoon. The bankers showed up promptly and we proceeded with small talk—the economy, the weather, how were we liking our new office, etc. My partner John attended with me but my other partner, although was there and invited, never left his desk—not sure what he was working on.

As the chit-chat reached its conclusion, the bankers handed us paperwork for signature that required all partners to sign new guarantees, saying this was the best and final offer to pay off our line of credit. We would make four equal monthly payments with the final being paid off by the end of the year. When we asked for time to think about it, they told us the offer was open until close of business the next day (Friday) whereby if we did not sign, the bank would move to close on the existing guarantees and initiate an action for judgment.

During the meeting I was interrupted by our financial director, who needed to speak with me for a minute. It was rare for her to interrupt a meeting, so I excused myself. Besides, I could let her know the terms we were going to need to live by.

"Craig, the bank has frozen our accounts, as well as your personal account," she told me. I guess the bank was done negotiating. *Damn, I had been meaning to move my personal account to another bank.* Procrastination had bitten again.

I returned to the meeting and agreed that we would accept the terms and sign the next day. Leverage is tricky—you either have it or you don't. It is important to realize when negotiations have concluded.

Firing a Partner

I think I mentioned that after our founder resigned I had two partners. John and one other, whom I don't speak about too much as he was never around and didn't help at all. As the going got tough, he began pulling away from the firm. I later found out that while we were struggling to rebuild the company, working without pay, and working on projects to keep a small amount of cash coming in, he was busy doing side work and keeping himself busy. He was a great designer and had been with us for a very long time. But when we needed him most, he showed his true colors. I remember talking to John about it several years later, who remarked that he had seen it coming for years, but that he didn't want to put any more pressure on me at the time.

After the bankers left, John and I walked to the back of the office to find out why our other partner had not attended the meeting. He said that he didn't need to be there and was busy on a deadline. Okay.

We explained the situation to him. The bank had attached our account. This account had money that was scheduled to be paid to the consultants. We explained the terms of the payoff and that we had no choice. We would all need to sign on the new agreement. Much to my surprise, our partner said he would not sign on the note unless we gave him additional stock in the company. I was incensed. At our company's lowest point, when we needed to bond together as partners, we were being leveraged from within. I'm sure I dropped a series of "F-bombs" that day.

I stepped back and tried to place myself in his shoes. No, I couldn't do it. I could not be that selfish. John and I walked away and decided that enough was indeed enough. We scheduled a meeting for Saturday to discuss further. I called my attorney and asked if his demand was a violation of our partner agreement and was pleased to find out that it was. On Friday, I called the bank to find out if it would be acceptable that if for some reason, we only had two partners who both signed. The bank didn't care, as long as all owners were on the hook.

I didn't sleep well Friday night. I tossed and turned, running over scenarios in my head. I never liked conflict but I knew what needed to be done. My other partner was a big guy, kind of intimidating, and I was a bit worried. But John would be with me and I knew we would be up for the challenge.

John and I arrived early for the meeting that fateful Saturday. Our other partner arrived and after getting coffee, we settled down at our high-top table—a gift from our next door neighbor, a furniture dealer. Originally lent to us, the dealer decided that we could keep it. What a nice table! I could stand or sit on a barstool at the table. That day, I chose to sit.

John and I proceeded to 'do the deed.' We told our partner why we could not go forward together anymore. We cited our partnership agreement as requiring us to sign on notes when the company needed us to do so. We told him we did not appreciate his absence during the last year or him leveraging us for additional stock to make this loan work. We said we wanted him to pack up his personal items and leave that day. Much to my surprise, he accepted it; he packed his stuff and walked out the door. We got his keys and told him to think about what he wanted to do about his car, which the company owned. We said he could continue making the payments and keep it.

I cannot tell you the relief I felt as I watched him leave the office for the last time. I felt authentic, true to the values of our company, and I knew we did the right thing for both him and us. The next day John and I talked and both of us were happy that another chapter in the history of the firm had been turned. We were poised for success.

When we arrived at the office on Monday, our former partner's car was in the parking lot. In the office were the keys and a note saying he did not want the car, which he dropped off earlier in the day. One of our staff was there to receive the envelope, and thank God he had the decency not to say anything about the events of the weekend.

The Monday morning staff meeting was a great time to let everyone know what had just transpired. For the most part, the staff were not surprised in the least, with one exclaiming, "About time!" We soon discovered the staff had been referring to him as the cancer that would eventually eat us all alive. He was a true seagull manager—you know, the one who flies in, shits on everything, and flies away. They were happy to see him gone.

Looking back, there were so many signs that he wasn't the right partner for us but I ignored them. I was blinded by his talent and fearful that we didn't have the design capacity to push us to the next level—a belief that has proven not to be true in the slightest.

Another lesson learned the hard way. When someone shows you who they really are, believe it. I'm not sure who coined this phrase, but it is brilliant.

The Other Shoe Drops

John and I always talked about the setbacks we faced as 'the other shoe dropping.' We became accustomed to knowing that the process would be two steps forward and one step backward. But what happened in December of 2012 was devastating to me personally as well as to the firm.

We had paid off the line of credit, were steadily paying off the consultant notes, and had even picked up a new project. With our partnership down to just John and me, we felt so optimistic about where we had been and where we were going. We had just started to transition our accounts to the new bank when I received a phone call.

"Craig? This is Julie."

"Hi Julie; how's it going?"

"Not too good. I have a rare bone cancer and will need to leave the firm to take care of myself."

Julie had been with us since the late 1990s. She was our financial director, our rock, and our confidant. She was one of my closest friends in the firm. She was instrumental in my leadership arc and taught me just about everything I knew about finance, banking, accounting, and managing cashflow. She believed in me and that was what I needed most becoming a new leader.

I thought something had been wrong. Julie lived in Idaho, and was our first experiment in remote work, well before anyone else was doing it. She used to visit Las Vegas once a month to connect with us but for the past couple of months had not been able to. Little did I know that she was seeking treatment for a sore hip and leg, something she thought was muscular. Once we found out John and I called her daily, offering support and just being her friend.

January 2013 brought new challenges. Without Julie running our financials, John and I were like fish out of water. While we were much better businessmen than we were a year ago, we could not access our accounting software and we could not find the accounting records for the current projects. Julie's son mailed us the files and once received, we realized that we hadn't billed since November. We received notice that our healthcare had not been renewed. I'll never forget personally taking a handwritten check to the healthcare administrator and pleading for reinstatement.

The anxiety attacks returned. I hadn't had one in a few months so it caught me off guard. I remember telling John, "We worked so hard to pay off debt, get new work, and now we are going under because we can't account for it all!"

Eventually we got lucky and found someone to come in to help us part time. She really saved us. We audited every project, every transaction, and eventually got everything on track. We needed her and she needed the extra money—a match made in heaven.

When you have a small company, staff are like family. We truly enjoyed being around each other. That was especially true for our group. We were a special bunch, bound together through adversity and optimistic about the future.

Julie passed later in March of 2013. She was a great woman we loved and miss her still!

Grit to Great

It's not easy to look back on this time in my life when I was trying to keep a firm alive, with a chance for failure at every turn. But telling the story has helped me see the positive things I learned in this time of crisis. I know I am better for having lived through these difficult times and will be better prepared for the future.

In 2015, Linda Kaplan Thaler and Robin Koval released the book, *Grit to Great*. It encapsulated my life and the struggles I had gone through in 2011 and 2012. The subtitle, *How Perseverance, Passion, and Pluck take you from Ordinary to Extraordinary*, was my anthem. I only wish I could've read the book in the fall of 2011, as it would've fueled my confidence to stick it out even more, but we had done the best we could. The moment I read the book in 2015, it resonated with me because I had indeed lived it.

There are so many lessons learned in the book. I will only be able to summarize a few here. I recommend that you pick up a copy for yourself and your team. Read it together and talk about the lessons learned. Your perspective of success will change.

Hard Work Trumps Talent

Working harder than those with more talent often leads to greater results. I found that the harder I worked, the better outcomes happened. While I think I always worked harder than most, I can definitely tell you that during our crisis, we worked harder than we had in a long time. There were many late nights, and I believe John and I worked every single Saturday for a year and a half to make sure we were on top of things. While we were working on solving the big issues, we were also responsible for the day-to-day marketing, management, and firm leadership. Looking back, it felt like we were working two jobs—keeping things current/moving forward, and fixing the sins of the past.

My advice to you regarding working hard is to also make some time for yourself. I will talk further about this topic in another chapter, but you MUST take some time off for you, your family, and slow the inevitable burnout.

Mix Passion and Patience

Passion will get you through many things, but you must be patient as well. This proved to be particularly true—and especially difficult—for me. I had set a schedule for recovery, but it seemed that every time I reached a milestone there was another setback or issue outside of my control. I have never been a patient person, but this time in my life taught me that things were not always going to happen on my timetable. I'm reminded that greater people than I have struggled with things not going their way—and they learned how to accept setbacks. I'm reminded of a famous Thomas Edison quote regarding his work on the lightbulb.

When a person asked him, "How did it feel to fail 1,000 times?" Edison replied, "I didn't fail 1,000 times. The light bulb was an invention with 1,000 steps."

"Great success is built on failure, frustration, even catastrophe."

When I played baseball, one of the adages our coaches taught us was to not let failure in one at-bat ruin our chance for success in the next at-bat. This was very true in our business; we couldn't let our current setback impair our ability to move forward on the solution. Each at-bat taught us something about the next pitch to be thrown our way.

Stay Determined Throughout Hardships

I think passion can lead to determination. As I mentioned previously, we were focused on paying off our debts and doing the 'right' thing. This mindset helped us stay focused during the hardships and setbacks. It was this determination to succeed that led to us actually succeed when many times it would have been easier to throw in the towel.

"Never get outworked by anyone!"

Thanks, Dad.

LESSON TWO

STAY TRUE TO YOUR VALUES

LESSON TWO

Stay True to Your Values

"The dark night of the soul comes just before revelation.
When everything is lost, and all seems darkness, then comes the new life and all that is needed."

Joseph Campbell, *Reflections on the Art of Living*

In the early 2000s, my mentor gave me the book, *Reflections on the Art of Living* by Joseph Campbell. I read it then but during my crisis, it became a source of inspiration and wisdom unlike before. Still today, whenever I feel down or anxious, reading a few passages from this book rejuvenates my mind and calms my soul.

I have always lived as a man of integrity and values. I believed that I acted within those solid morals and values and modeled this behavior for others, especially to my wife and children. What I learned from the difficult times in the recession of 2011–2014 gave me even more purpose. I was able to demonstrate and confirm the things in which

I believe through my actions. I learned about myself, how I would handle difficult situations, loss, and how to really model behavior around values.

While what a leader says does matter, how a leader acts is even more important. Actions can either reinforce or undermine the words that are said. Every time you have an opportunity—even small—to live and act in accordance with the things you hold true, it builds your capacity as a leader. I didn't realize it at the time, but over the course of my career I was groomed to be a good leader. From picking up trash on the floor, to being transparent in decision making, to questioning other's actions, I was living my values and demonstrating to others that it mattered.

Honesty Really is the Best Policy

It seems like such a cliché, but honesty has always been the best policy. The more honest we were with our staff, our consultants, our bank, and ourselves, the more time and resources we were given to solve the problems at hand. We easily could have been sued, been exposed to our clients for not paying our bills, or had our note called by our bank. But none of those things happened because we were honest with people and demonstrated that we were working hard to solve the problems we created.

We were transparent with our staff—they knew the magnitude of the problem and also knew how important they were to the solution. Every week we updated them on our progress. We felt it was very important that they knew the company was trending upward, so we shared our financials in monthly office meetings. This was unheard of in our industry. People thought we were crazy, but we were trying to rebuild a company and this was our way of demonstrating how tight cash was, when we could plan to have our salaries restored, and how long it would take to pay off the debt. We treated our staff as partners in this journey and they responded that way.

Of that I am proud.

I had never worked at a company this open to its staff. In hindsight, while I think that was the best thing we could have done at the time, it was a little too much information for some to handle. When someone doesn't know the basic building blocks of business—costs, overhead, indirect salary expenses, etc.—it is difficult to get on the same page. If I were to do it again, I would most likely hold some of the information closer to the vest and just share the overall monthly financial trending of the organization. I realized that staff does care, but cannot care in the same way as the owners. Staff really just needed assurance that they would have a job to come to each morning, and that they could practice their craft and make a dent in the universe. I'm saddened that we lost a couple of people back then because they couldn't understand our honesty and openness. The point is, however, even when you do the things you think are right, they will not always be interpreted that way. You need to become comfortable with that.

One of the most honest things any leader can do is be honest with himself (or herself). Real leaders know themselves and are completely honest about their strengths and weaknesses. This is so important, as it allows a leader to align with those whose strengths are his or her weaknesses to augment leadership capacity and spur growth. It is not easy. Being honest with yourself takes work, but it is work that yields great results. It takes many hours of contemplation and a realization that you cannot "fake it until you make it."

I felt the best way to fully understand my strengths was to talk to others. I had an idea of what my strengths were but getting confirmation from others was very helpful. When I revealed that I felt I was weak in a certain area, something magical happened. People offered help, books to read, or just encouragement. When a leader reveals himself, he gains respect and status in the eyes of others—and access to myriad resources. But he also gains permission to be vulnerable and not have all of the answers, which by the way, we never have.

The key to developing into an authentic leader lies in being honest with yourself so that you can learn where you need to grow. In order to understand who I really was, I found that reviewing my life-shaping events to understand what was learned or how I reacted was extremely helpful. This was instrumental in becoming comfortable with who I was. I reviewed how I reacted to my first job, my first love, my marriage, my children, the ups and downs of being married, losing my parents, early leadership experiences. I used a journaling technique to break these down and identify the highs and lows of my life. It was cumbersome work and I filled a ton of notebooks, but each word I wrote and each thought I had moved me closer to authentically understanding myself. Understanding one's tendencies is very important as you continue the valuable work on yourself.

I also spent a lot of time questioning my purpose. I was lucky in that I knew my life revolved around service; service to my family, service to my community, service to my clients, and service to my profession. It only made sense that my purpose of service to our firm made me a good leader. This drive to serve others and move the company forward fueled my passion and made it easy to come to work every day even in the worst of times. I wanted to keep our staff employed and dreamed of the days when I would get to see them have families, put their kids in college, and continue to grow and lead in the future. I know this is a very uncommon belief, but I also think that we form companies to organize and collect like-minded people to collaborate with. While most people think that companies are in business to make money, I believe people are in business to collectively serve clients, be great employers, and make our community a better place to live. When we do that, money finds us. The more we focused on the right things, the more profitable we became.

I truly focused on the needs of our staff and clients. It was very clear to me that they needed us and we needed them. Our clients hired us for the gifts we had and we responded immediately with gratitude and excitement. To be able to have a client during this time was a privilege and we cannot ever forget this. Also, to be able to maintain a quality staff so essential to the good work we were doing was both humbling and appreciated. Whenever times get tough now, I remember the glue that held us together, caring for the needs of others.

Be an Original

Our founding partner was an incredible visionary and inspirational leader. When I first met him, I knew he had an innate ability to think deeply and see the future of business. He and I had similar visions of what the company of the future could look like—a collegial group of people working with purpose and conviction, focused on improving our community. We spoke of the concept of creating a company so engaging that people would show up every day and pay would be secondary to purpose. We wanted volunteers, but we also wanted to pay them well. We believed that profit and people's salaries were like oxygen; necessary to live but not the reason that people came to work.

He had a way of seeing things that others could not see in the marketplace and communicate large and inspirational goals to all of us, but he was not the best at putting strategies or plans in place to achieve these goals. That is where I came in. I could make good plans and determine the steps to implement those big ideas. We were a good pair and the more I was able to implement the ideas, the grander the ideas became. We did some amazing work, and built systems and a practice model that still anchors us today and differentiates us from our competitors.

When the founding partner resigned in fall of 2011, I found myself in a quandary. I was always looked at as the strategy and implementation guy in the firm. Who would be the visionary?

The breakup of our partnership was very painful for me. I felt betrayed. This betrayal reached its pinnacle when the last time my partner and I spoke on the phone, he told me he thought we could not survive without his visionary leadership and if we did survive as a company, we would be just another 'me-too' architectural firm. Those words cut deep. In our culture the words 'me-too' were used to describe the failures of our profession, the isomorphism and commoditization of architectural firms. One of our values was to be distinctive and differentiated in the marketplace, the opposite of 'me-too.' I know today that his comments became deeply important for me to prove wrong and may have been the fuel that helped keep me going during incredibly tough times.

With our founder gone, I felt that I needed to be the visionary leader he was. I felt I needed to replace him, which by all accounts was impossible. I tried everything from reading visionary leadership books to holding vision sessions within the firm. Over the next year what I realized was that I was visionary but different, and that was okay. I didn't need to replace my former partner; the firm needed me to be me. Just because I had played the role of strategist and implementer, this did not define me. I could and would grow to be a complete leader, but I could be an original, too. To this day, I believe I am not as visionary as my former partner, but my belief in the value of vision moves me forward every day.

Vision is an interesting thing. It can drive an organization forward, but it can also have a detrimental effect. Not everyone sees the vision the same, which is healthy, as long as we all realize that we are not looking for solid 'yes-people' in our organization. We are looking for enough overlap in our belief system to hang together. It does not need to be absolute. In our firm's previous history, belief and understanding of our vision was used to judge people and determine if they were the 'right fit.' While I still look for good overlap and belief in something bigger than ourselves, I am committed to being more inclusive and open to others' perspectives. When we can keep from judging people without clearly having the dialogue and understanding of each other, we create a much more vibrant and exciting organization to be a part of. The diversity of thought is a gift to your company.

My good friend Alex Raffi wrote the book *Creative Courage*, with the premise being that we are all creative; the creative process is not mutually exclusive and is readily available for anyone to access. This is another highly recommended book as it will help you understand that creativity can be learned, practiced, and grown.

Over the tough years, I began to believe more in the process of vision and less in the reliance on the person as being visionary. It's similar to creativity; the process to develop a vision is readily available and can be harnessed for our good and the good of our company. Just like creativity, we all have it and can see things bigger than ourselves. I needed to learn this the hard way and now realize that sound processes unlock visionary thinking.

Vision is not reliant upon a person.

Years later one of my friends gave me the book, *Originals*, by Adam Grant. Another great read and another resource for you as you continue your leadership journey. The book breaks the myths that leaders are born, and that you need to be a conformist to succeed. Grant demonstrates that you can find strength in your weaknesses and that everyone can have a major impact on their company. The world really needs us to be ourselves and surround ourselves with those whose strengths complement ours to fill the voids of our weaknesses. I will talk extensively about that in another chapter, but for now, don't be afraid to be an original and recognize your gifts to the world.

Follow Through on Your Promises

One of our consultants was very difficult to deal with at first. He was also the one we owed the most and he was still working on some of our projects. When I first called him to express that I knew we had the problem and were working on a solution, I could tell that he did not believe we would make good on the debt. I will refer to him as 'Dave.' Dave was a good engineer, and in my opinion a very good businessman, someone I looked up to. I was also intimidated by him as I was very vulnerable at this time in my life. We owed Dave's company a significant amount of money and I knew the only way I could pay it back was over a long time.

After the first call, when I told Dave I needed a little time to formulate a plan, I opened up Pandora's box. Dave called me every day thereafter and the typical conversation went like this.

Me: Hello.

Dave: Do you have my money?

Me: I'm working on it.

Dave: Are you going to have it tomorrow?

Me: No, but in a few weeks I will have a plan.

Dave: Talk to you tomorrow.

This call went on daily for about ten days. It was very stressful to me and I thought many times of not answering the phone, but felt that would make things worse. Finally I exploded!

Me: Hello.

Dave: Do you have my money?

Me: Dave, what do you want me to say?

Dave: That you have my money.

Me: Dave, I promise that we will pay you back everything we owe you.

Dave: With interest?

Me: Dave, I know we created the problem, but hounding me every day is not going to solve the problem. What I need is you to allow me the time to put together a plan to pay you back. I'm thinking it will be over at least two years.

Dave: If it's going to take that long to get paid, I'm going to need interest on top of the debt.

Me: I think we can agree to something like this.

Dave: Okay, send something over to sign.

Me: Dave, what I really need is for you to be in my camp, root me on, be my friend, and know that we are really trying to put this behind us. It would be much easier for our firm to fail or declare bankruptcy, but then everyone loses. I can start payments in two months.

Dave: Okay. We'll judge this on your monthly performance.

I spoke to my partner John about what I had just committed to and he agreed with me. While I can't tell you I really felt much better or any sense of relief, I can say that I looked forward to not getting the call from Dave the next day.

I sent the note over to Dave shortly and he signed and returned it. Now we had to concentrate on making the first payment. John and I knew it was most likely coming out of our salaries. There is something to be said about dealing with your problems straight up. While it doesn't make it easy, the feeling of authenticity is somewhat exhilarating.

Those two months went by very quickly and the day came to send the first payment to Dave. We made the payment and something magical happened.

Me: Hello.

Dave: Hey, Craig, we received your payment.

Me: Good, glad it got there on time.

Dave: Hey, Craig, I'm rooting for you guys. You are one of the good ones and I hope you can get this turned around and start making some money for your company in addition to paying off our debt. Keep up the good work.

After the second payment:

Me: Hello.

Dave: Hey, Craig, we received your payment.

Me: Good, glad it got there on time.

Dave: Hey, Craig, I'm rooting for you guys. You are one of the good ones and I hope you can get this turned around and start making some money for your company in addition to paying off our debt. Keep up the good work.

Dave called me every month after we had made the payment with similar words of encouragement. I can tell you that I actually looked forward to hearing from Dave. He truly became one of our biggest supporters during that time. I remember the calls fondly. Diligently, we made the payments to Dave and the other consultants each and every month.

I was super excited when we made the final payment to Dave. The payment represented 2.5 years of working hard. I felt fulfilled and the company was turning around. One of the toughest situations was being viewed in the rear view mirror. Dave called and invited me to lunch to celebrate the final payment.

We met at a nice Italian restaurant, chit-chatted about families, vacation, business, and ordered our food. I ordered a small pizza and salad. I remember because I very rarely ate large lunches, but this was a special day. I had no idea how special, however.

While the waiter was gone getting our order, Dave reached down into his briefcase and handed our last check to me. He said, "Here is the interest back!" Not expecting this show of kindness, I broke into tears. I told him that I couldn't accept the check as the interest was really owed to him for our mistake.

He said, "Craig, eight firms owed me money during the recession. Your firm is the only one that handled it professionally and the only one that paid us back. You are the only one who made good on your promise and for that I have the ultimate respect for you and your firm. Please accept this gesture and a thank you for being so honest and committed."

I didn't need this show of gratitude, but it sure felt good. Dave recognized how difficult this situation was for our firm and appreciated us. I think I broke into a good cry on the way back to the office and felt as good as I had felt in a very long time.

We did the right thing.

I wrote a blog several years ago about how our ability to keep promises has eroded as a society, little by little. It's worthy of repeating here:

> *I've learned over the course of my career that there are soft promises and hard promises. Soft promises are those we don't really have to fulfill.*

I'm sure that many times as you were leaving a function, you told someone you'd call for lunch or to go golfing, knowing that you'd probably forget or not call. The other party knew it, too, but there was no real consequence for not keeping the promise. We all make these kinds of promises and because both parties know that the promise won't be kept, this behavior is culturally acceptable.

A hard promise is one that, when not fulfilled, has a negative consequence. If you tell someone you'll deliver a project by a certain time or attend an important meeting, there are ramifications if you don't follow through. Not only is your reputation affected, but your relationships can be damaged.

So why don't people keep the hard promises? One reason is that some people let the daily task list get in the way of the promises previously made. We live in a fast-paced world where there is always something urgent to do. Another reason is that over time people desensitize themselves to the importance of fulfilling hard promises by habitually not fulfilling the soft ones. Once you establish an attitude that devalues the soft promises, your perspective on hard promises can erode as well. It is a vicious cycle and one that can erode your career.

Here are some things to consider in helping you keep your promises:

Practice discipline. People who have fallen into the trap of not fulfilling promises aren't bad people. They have just become undisciplined in their thoughts and actions. They have become accustomed to telling people what they think they want to hear and less accustomed to considering the implications of the promises they make. This creates a slippery slope that takes discipline to climb. Taking the time necessary to understand what you are committing to will allow you to make better decisions, and in turn, better promises.

Words matter. I'm sure that not a single one of us would tell a client, "I'm going to deliver your project two days later than I tell you." Yet many of us do deliver late, violating the promise. Think of your actions in terms of the promise given; make a promise you are sure you can keep.

Stay focused on important things. Each day we are hit with many things to do. Our task list grows out of proportion with the actual urgency of these tasks. Stay focused on the items that are truly important to you and your clients. I suggest rather than just keeping a to-do list, develop a promise list and hold this to a high level of importance. Be careful of how many promises you make. Take a critical look at your list and be honest: can you really commit to this new promise?

People don't trust those who don't fulfill their promises. Have you ever been in a meeting

> *where a chronic underperformer promises to*
> *do something? You can almost hear people's*
> *eyes rolling back. Everyone is thinking, "yeah,*
> *right, sure." Don't become the one who loses*
> *trust of others by not keeping your promises.*
> *It takes a lot of work to regain someone's trust.*

So simply stated the lesson here is ... keep your promises or don't make them.

Communication

I can't state strongly enough that communication skills are the most important skills that all business leaders need to develop. Think of it: almost every problem you face has an element of miscommunication or misunderstanding. Learning to communicate effectively and using inquiry to confirm that the message is heard can save you countless hours dealing with the ramifications of an issue.

Communication is a two-way street. To be able to communicate effectively, one must also become a good listener. Ask questions to make sure you have heard things correctly, and when you are communicating, ask the other party to paraphrase back to you what you said. This will identify gaps in the process and lead to a deeper dialogue and eventual understanding. Practice delivering your message just like you would practice if you were giving a speech or presentation. Practice can improve your message and your delivery.

Another thing I've found is that delivering important messages need to have the right setting and can't be rushed. Too often, we don't schedule enough time to talk with people and by the time we get past the small talk to really discuss the point, we run out of time and rush it. Effective communication takes time; don't shortchange the process.

Communication should be something you value.

The Rise of New Policies

In the architecture business, almost 50 percent of the work we do for clients is completed by consultants or vendor/ partners who work under our contract. Our job is to design the project, coordinate our specialists' work and ensure that a full set of design documents is completed. Consultant work is important to the overall project and their fees are run through our office.

Knowing that we got the firm into trouble in 2010 and 2011, John and I vowed it would never happen again. One of the most successful policies was to open a separate checking account that was only used for paying our consultants. When we receive payment from our client, we deposit the portion of the fee owed to consultants into this special checking account, removing the co-mingling of our fees with our consultants. This allows us to be able to know exactly what we owe each one of our partners and always have their money available when they invoice.

Since this account is used only for paying our consultants, and not co-mingled with anything else, we never see the balance and do not consider these funds in making any decisions. It helps us focus on our company and forces us to make hard decisions when we need to.

This policy has served us well and we are very proud that we will never be in the same predicament as previously. An unexpected outcome of our new policy recently resulted in our firm receiving a new project. A client contacted us who said they wanted to move a project from another firm to us. Apparently that firm was not paying its consultants on time and one of the consultants recommended that they move the project to us since we had such a good track record. This validation was much appreciated. I only hope the other firm learns the way we did and develops new policies to move themselves forward.

In addition to paying more attention to the financial systems in the firm, we have significantly ramped up our marketing system. We spent a number of years just surviving and although we did some good work over that period of time, we lost our way in terms of brand perception. We were doing work that was not a good representation of our brand and during the recession, many of our clients changed jobs, retired, or moved away, so we were only recognized for what we were doing currently and not our previous brand position.

One of the first things that Brittany, our new marketing director suggested was to conduct a client perception survey. I was shocked at the results; some clients said they only thought of us for small renovation projects, and some said they thought we did good work, but did not know what projects would be a good fit. We knew we had some work to do. We were previously known as one of the most sustainable and community-minded architecture firms in our city.

We needed to change our mindset from survive to thrive. What type of projects would we want to be working on if we had the choice? We had months of discussion of where our gifts would be best used and we needed to learn how to say "no" to certain clients and projects. When you live in a survival mindset, you think of the world as a zero-sum game; you must take everything and never say no to projects. That is so detrimental to an organization long term. Over the years, from 2015 to now, we have gotten really good at saying no appropriately and letting clients know where we would be the best fit.

A good friend of mine coined the phrase "an RFQ is not a subpoena; you don't need to respond." That is so true. Only pursue the work that is fulfilling and the projects that will propel you forward to your desired vision. We decided that our firm was best suited to working on projects that had actual clients who would occupy the facility. Therefore, speculative retail or office/industrial work did not fit the bill. We are a purpose-centered practice and we work best with clients who share that same ethic. This mindset eventually helped us gravitate to public community work, non-profit organizations, and education. Our preferred projects included museums, libraries, interpretive centers, parks, recreation centers, churches, and schools. These are good fits and connected to our values and brand.

We revised our website, our approach to business development, which organizations we belong to and invest our energy, and changed our whole presentation strategy to fit with the work we wanted. This was a tedious process but exciting and transformational to our firm, and it is paying dividends.

Everything worth doing is worth doing consistent with what you value.

LESSON THREE

LEADERSHIP IS A TEAM SPORT

LESSON THREE

Leadership is a Team Sport

When I was growing up I loved playing baseball. I still love watching baseball and appreciate the nuance of the game. When you are young, you learn to play all the positions but as you progress, you find the best position that uses your gifts. The same is true of your team's batting order. You'd never put your home-run hitter up first; you need the guys who can walk or hit singles to set the table for the bigger hitters. Baseball is a great team sport calculated in both individual and team stats.

Leadership is similar to baseball. It requires individual strengths in many different areas. It also requires many skills and teammates to perform those functions. I hear many people say that leadership is lonely, and I thought that at first. However, I've learned that leadership is not lonely if you set up a great team. If you look at many of history's great leaders you will find that they were all supported by other great people whose skills complemented the leaders' weaknesses. Abraham Lincoln may be the extreme example of this. In the book, *Team of Rivals*, Doris Kearns Goodwin exposes one of the keys to Lincoln's success—his mastery of organizing a team that supported and made his leadership stronger.

This is true of leading a company. No one can have all the skills and expertise required. Even if there is a leadership savant among us, he or she certainly does not have the time to devote to everything. Building a team that you trust will help you immensely; it will create a place for diversity of thought and will engage ideas and make them achievable. But make sure you build a team of people with different opinions, skills, and interests, and a team that is not afraid to disagree with you. If Lincoln was able to build a team of rivals into a cohesive group, you can certainly build a team of advisors from your allies.

The Servant as Leader

If you have followed or read anything about leadership, then you no doubt have heard of Robert Greenleaf and/or "The Servant as Leader." This essay was written in 1970 and is still one of my go-to reads, although I have the 1991 version. Mr. Greenleaf's premise is that it is through service that leadership is bestowed. Those who remain true to service find many opportunities to lead.

I always believed I was put on this earth to serve, with service to my family, my community, and my profession part and parcel of my personal creed. But what I learned about service during the most difficult time in our firm's history to date will never be forgotten. I immediately noticed how those around me were struggling with the uncertainty of the recession and whether or not they would be employed in the near future. This stress was too much for some people to bear and I sensed that they wanted to help but couldn't figure out how.

While I became a servant to my company, I was really putting myself in a position, through service, to help protect the few jobs left and re-grow the company back to a viable and fruitful organization that would take care of us all. John and I clearly knew that our employees and their families relied upon our each and every action. That motivated us to put in the time demonstrating a service model that put our people at the center. Our firm had always been very purpose-centered, but we realized the importance of being even more intentional with how we engaged and how our work aligned with this purpose. If people are going to stick with you and your firm during difficult times, it will be because they get to work on something meaningful that connects to their purpose.

My role as the servant was to fill their plate with opportunities so that they could practice architecture and make a difference. At the same time, John and my roles were also to insulate them from the stress of the business so they could focus on their work. By serving our staff's needs, we were able to build a strong, trusting culture again.

Several years later I gave a talk to a marketing group about leadership qualities, preparation, and styles. After the talk, one of the attendees sent me a book by Kenneth R. Jennings and John Stahl-Wert titled *The Serving Leader*. Another great read and another book I wished would've been available in 2011. If it's not in your library, it should be!

In *The Serving Leader*, Jennings and Stahl-Wert describe in detail what John and I learned. By connecting our staff around a purpose, and through serving the company and their needs, we have been able to achieve great things and build the tightest group of employees we have ever had in our firm's long and storied history. That is no small feat.

When others see you in service to them, they take notice and follow.

Being recognized for service to your company opens up many possibilities, including others in your organization offering to help where they see fit. Exposing yourself to your organization allows people to see the 'real' you and affords them the foresight to see where and how they can best help you. Being of service begets service as well.

Building the Bridge as You Walk on it.

Change is hard. It is hard for us personally and especially difficult for a company with so many differing opinions and situations. The key to managing change is to get buy-in on a collective vision, grounded in purpose, and connect to inspirational and aspirational goals. I have written about this previously, but I learned that you cannot separate personal change from organizational change as one influences the other. To effect organizational change, one must embrace personal change. The more I studied leadership and organizational change, the more I changed personally and the more prepared I became to lead change in the organization.

During this time period I learned the analogy of building a bridge while you walk on it. It is a perfect metaphor for organizational change. Organizational change takes time, and during the process the organization has one foot in the past, a foot in the present, and a longing to take the step to the future. With each step, one sheds the past and reaches out again to the future. Although this sounds very incremental and deliberate, it does not always feel that way. Sometimes the steps to the future feel like huge leaps; other times the past clings to your foot like thick mud and drags you back. But forward is the operative direction for positive change.

Once we had gotten the firm back on a path to positive financial footing it was time to begin charting our path forward. We engaged our strategic partner, 'Imagine Communications,' to conduct interviews of each of our staff and provide a report of things we needed to work on. We also conducted a client survey to understand their perceptions of the firm.

Based on the reports and surveys, we found we had some work to do. Our employees had suffered greatly over the past three to four years. Some had psychological wounds and others couldn't drop their baggage and feelings from the past. In addition, many of the clients we had worked with over the years had either retired or moved to other organizations. This proved problematic in the survey results as the people who filled out the surveys only knew us for the work we were currently doing and not for the years of work prior to the recession. Our brand had been almost instantly reshaped.

Both of these issues need to be addressed quickly and differently. We scheduled an 'all hands and hearts' meeting in the summer of 2013 to address the issues of our people. Through a series of sessions over the next few months, we worked through the major issues of trust, which resulted in a more connected workplace. In hindsight, the fact that we demonstrated that we cared for employee wellbeing paid dividends. Our people just needed to talk and we needed to listen. It was healing and we learned a lot to springboard us to the future.

We initiated a series of visioning sessions where we had the opportunity to craft a new direction for the firm. These sessions showed how connected we really were around the things that mattered. The sessions came off well, without pretenses. In the past, these type of sessions were met with resistance and sometimes even outright back stabbing. Not with this group. I was feeling great that we are not only on the right path financially, but also culturally.

One particularly gratifying area was our alignment around core values. We had long discussions around the values we held closely and vetted them thoroughly, proving that we indeed did all believe in them. We used actions to demonstrate the values and each person in the organization was empowered to call each other out when we were not acting within the value set we said we believed in. Our office was built around care and empathy and we held each other accountable to these standards.

Re-building the Brand

Our new vision allowed for a connection to who we were but really jumped us to who we could become. The goals of the organization grew from the vision and we began implementing them carefully and deliberately. One area we focused on was getting back to building strong relationships with our present clients and future clients. We developed a stronger business development culture by ranking the clients we wanted to keep and assigning staff members to make sure we stayed connected with each one. We identified a champion and a second baseman for each client. In addition, we collectively began more focused business development check-ins and pushed business development to everyone in the office, making it not just my responsibility. I still took the lead and focused my time on new pursuits. Our marketing director encouraged us to be more focused on the type of work we could bring great value to.

Many firms shotgun their business development approach. They chase projects and believe that through sheer volume they will be successful. We took a very different approach. We did not want to be a client collector, but more of a curator. We targeted the types of clients and projects where we believed we had the most alignment and could bring the most value. We then set out to meet each client and show them who we were, what we cared about, and most importantly, why. We prepared special presentations that connected our past work to our future endeavors and we shared our values and what type of projects we believed we could do best for them. We also stated which ones we didn't believe were good fits and developed a strong culture around what projects were best and how to say 'no' the right way.

These were exciting times in our firm and as we have now added new partners, things are really clicking. I'm most proud of how our team connected and made a difference in the lives of our clients and who we were designing for. A new website, a new strategy, and a new way to differentiate our firm came from our ability to embrace change.

When people align around a strong purpose, nothing will stop them from succeeding and building that bridge to the future, even while they have one foot in the past.

Care and Empathy

During our vision discussions and subsequently through our work, we became even more clear that we cared for our clients and their endeavors. I know this sounds cliché; who would ever say they didn't care? But for us this was different.

Our new success was built from our ability to demonstrate our care and truly develop empathy for our clients and their clients and patrons. Our marketing director challenged us then and each day forward to demonstrate our care or quit saying it.

It is funny to me that I always thought that was one of our distinctions, but our actions did not always show it. I realized later that we had serious disconnects in our previous partnerships and didn't align our actions with our beliefs. We were not authentic and the more authentic we became, the more the marketplace rewarded us. One of the cornerstones of designing great places is having an ability to step into our clients' and their clients' shoes. We need to be able to take diverse points of view and understand the varying needs of these people as they interact with what we design. It is not for the timid, as it takes a lot of work and at times can be overwhelming.

There is a shadow side to care and empathy. Sometimes we care too much. One cannot care about a project or an engagement more than the client does. The result is disappointing and leads to a disconnected engagement. It is a fine line to walk. For us, it has become critical to pick our clients well because when we don't, while we may still create a great project, the engagement is not fulfilling. And life is too short to work just for the money. Our teams and our collective firm need to work on things that make a difference, and it is through developing empathy and careful and thoughtful design we are able to do that.

A Confidant

con·fi·dant

noun
noun: confidant; plural noun: confidants;
noun: confidante; plural noun: confidantes

a person with whom one shares a secret or
private matter, trusting them not to repeat it to
others. "… a close confidante of the princess"

I have been happily married since 1983. Through thick and thin, my wife has always been my confidant, with each of us helping the other through the challenges of life. What I went through during this time in my firm's life required me to find an additional confidant. While my wife was still always there for me, I really did not want the problems of my company to be the sole conversations between us. And I needed to talk a lot about what I was going through.

I never thought I would need an additional confidant beyond my wife, but this time I did.

I have two younger brothers, both with whom I have a great relationship. I love them both and they have always been there for me. My brother Scott lives in Sacramento and my brother Todd lives in Reno/Sparks. We grew up close and I am incredibly proud of both of them, their accomplishments, and their families. As the oldest, I never wanted to burden either of them with my issues. In old Italian families, the oldest son is viewed as the padrone of the family, especially once the father passes. The padrone role is the protector of the family, the advisor, the counsellor, and the 'boss.'

While we don't subscribe to this old school way, there is a certain respect shown to the oldest. The oldest is the leader, and does not need help, especially from the younger brothers. I was the one who helped them, not the other way around.

My brother Scott is an attorney and runs his own business. I initially called him for advice on a few legal issues that I was facing at the time, but instantly felt comfortable talking to him about all my problems. One thing I noticed quickly was that he had a great ability to listen and didn't try to make the issues his own or tell me his problems and how he had dealt with these things in the past. He just listened and let me talk. It was exactly what I needed. No one could really tell me what to do; I needed to figure it out by myself. What I needed was someone who would listen, not judge, and be in my corner. Scott became my confidant.

It is important to have a confidant during difficult times. It is hard to keep going when there is another challenge at every step of the way. You need someone to talk to who is different from your spouse, and different from your business partners. If you pick a good confidant who lets you get out what you need to, then you can be stronger and more of a leader in your firm.

My brother and I talked daily, sometimes just a quick check-in and sometimes for hours. It depended on what I needed on a given day. I'm still amazed how much time he gave me and I'm not sure I can ever equalize it for him, but I also know he's not keeping score. In one of our talks, he told me to keep pedaling. I wasn't sure what he meant.

Me: I'm not sure the concept of pedaling.

Scott: Do you believe you are heading in the right direction?

Me: Yes, I think so.

Scott: Do you believe that God will help you find your way?

Me: Yes.

Scott: Then your job is to keep pedaling the bike and stay focused on the forward movement; you have a lot of help with direction. We won't let you get off course.

That reassurance was incredibly important to me and every time we talked afterward, Scott ended the conversation with, "Keep pedaling." That simple phrase kept me focused for the day.

Over the years, Scott and I even grew closer. We promised that once my crisis was getting better and more manageable, we'd go do something fun. My brothers and I have had a Brother's Weekend every year since 1995. Even during the tough times, we would always meet up somewhere, play golf together, bbq, drink beer, and enjoy each other's company. We had a nice tradition and kept it moving forward through thick and thin. There are years when one of us couldn't afford it, there were times when we modified our weekend to simpler - the point is we never miss this time together.

But Scott had something bigger in mind. A few years prior, Scott and his family had visited the town where our grandparents lived in Sicily prior to them immigrating to the US. Scott showed up in the Town Square with pictures of my grandparents and other family members and began showing them around to some of the people hanging out in the Square. After a few hours, one of the older gentlemen identified himself in one of the pictures. It turns out he was one of our cousins and he took Scott and his family to meet others. One of the pictures showed a shrine with my Aunt standing in front of it. They took Scott to see the shrine which was built in memory of my grandfather, whom none of us had ever met as he passed away when my dad was young. My grandmother came back to Sicily after her husband passed and had the shrine commissioned. Scott met other cousins and vowed to rerun to the town of Longi and spend more time.

Scott proposed that we go to Sicily together and retrace our roots. My wife was excited about this opportunity and Scott's wife was also supportive of us going on this trip. We invited my youngest brother Todd but he was unable to go at this time.

The planning of the trip was almost as exciting as the trip itself, as it took my mind off everything I had been through. We planned to stay two weeks in Sicily, touring the entire island with the last week in the small mountain town of Longi.

Sicily is a beautiful place with an amazing history. It was an important island throughout history due to its strategic location and therefore was conquered by many different countries. There are architectural works of Germans, Spanish, Indians, Greeks, and Romans. This eclectic place shows off some of the most amazing buildings from temples to castles to ancient theaters. While the architecture is grand, Sicilians are a simple and proud people and the food and wine is different than found in mainland Italy, and every bit as delicious.

One of the highlights of the trip was the drive into Longi. We drove in from the east side of the island, around Mt. Etna, on a series of country roads. The trip was long as the roads were small and twisted and turned around the volcano. Several wineries and vineyards dotted the side of the mountain. The wine from theses vineyards were very different as the rich lava soil varied so much because of the lava flows over millions of years.

We crested a mountain pass and entered into a town called Galati Mamertino. While the name of the town suggested that my family had been from there, we could find no evidence that the Galati's hailed from here. As we passed through Galati Mamertino, the road went down steeply into the beautiful village of Longi. We met our cousins, all from my grandmother's side of the family. The Brancatelli's had lived in Longi as long as anyone could remember. We were able to see the shrine to my grandfather, spend several days drinking, eating, and getting to know our long lost relatives. While I could not speak fluent Italian or the Sicilian dialect, between my brother Scoot who could speak Italian and my cousin Mariateresa, who could speak English, we were able to converse and enjoy their company. My cousins and their families treated us like kings and made us feel completely at home. Their hospitality was legendary.

This trip was such a celebration of all I had gone through and I have my brother Scott to thank for it.

Partnerships

There is an old adage that it 'takes a village' to do anything worthwhile. This was proven to me time and time again during the tough years. My firm built some strong partnerships and friendships that will never go away. All businesses were struggling with the great recession and we banded together strongly. If there is one thing I miss from these times, it is the deep care we showed each other. One of the only things we had was each other and we spent time helping and receiving help at the same time from our partners. I want to highlight and thank a few of the partners who made a difference in my life and the life of our firm during these times.

Imagine Communications was our marketing and public relations firm. We had built a great relationship prior to the recession and they helped us with rebranding our firm and designing a new website. But they were more than that. Co-owners Brian Rouff and Alex Raffi are great business partners and true friends.

Each month I had coffee with either Brian or Alex, or both, and always came away with more than I went in with. Their ability to listen, offer advice, and help remind me of our strategic purpose was much appreciated and needed at that time in my life. When the recession hit us hard, even though they were also feeling the pinch, they worked for us at reduced rates and sometimes for nothing at all. You could not ask for much more from a partner and they were really instrumental in our firm's turnaround. Thanks guys.

I highlighted Meadows Bank in a previous chapter, but this chapter would not be complete without recognition of their contribution to our firm. I knew Arvind Menon from his work at another bank. Arvind had hired our firm and we designed a few branches for the bank. Then Arvind left the bank and I lost touch with him. I was so happy when I received correspondence that Arvind was part of a group that was starting a new bank, Meadows Bank. Las Vegas means meadows in Spanish and I have always loved the word play for the bank's name.

When I went to visit Arvind the first time at Meadows Bank, I immediately knew that this bank would be great for us. Here we are now ten years later and the bank has been a great partner. Much thanks to Arvind Menon, Brad Tope, Donna Meyer, and Patrick Sullivan.

In early 2014, we met Lora Hendricksen and Enrique Villar. They had just started Radioactive Productions, a videography consultancy. At that time, we desired to develop more video content and it was a perfect fit. They were a new start-up firm, and we needed their services. What I didn't realize at the time was how great a partner Radioactive would be. They helped us in getting our message out correctly, helped us develop content beyond our wildest dreams, and taught us much about capturing the moments early and often to build a database of video that could be stitched together whenever we needed something. Thanks Lora, Enrique, and Abdullah Alotaibi.

LGA was fortunate to have started a 401K plan back in the early 2000s. At the time, we selected the Investment Counsel Company to manage our account and create our investments. Notwithstanding the fact that they are great investment advisors and take care of our company's 401k plan like their own, Randy Garcia and Michelle Konstantarakis became great friends and advisors. Randy was so helpful in teaching me basic business acumen and was always there for me when I had a question. Michelle also became someone whom I could talk with during the good times and bad. Thanks Randy and Michelle, for your counsel.

Gary Krape, CPA, provided valuable insight and business coaching to me at the time I needed it most. Gary helped me negotiate our debt with the consultants and the bank and was always there to listen and teach. I really value our business relationship and friendship. Thanks Gary.

The point of this section is we are never in it alone. While we may be the one tasked with making decisions, it is critical to surround ourselves with key leaders who can teach us, coach us, and make us think. I never would have been able to accomplish the things I did without these partnerships.

LESSON FOUR

STAY POSITIVE

LESSON FOUR

Stay Positive

Staying positive in the face of adversity is paramount to your success. You cannot solve the problems at hand if you wallow in them. You must stand up above the problem and attack it for what it is—a challenge and an opportunity. Viewing these challenges as opportunities to grow will free you up to think strategically and move forward. During my baseball days I remember being taught to go up to the plate loose and free. Just like one cannot play baseball when you grip the bat too tight, developing a looseness in your work will pay dividends.

I wish I could tell you that during the winter of 2011–2012, I was loose and approached my problems with the confidence and swagger that I approach them with now, but that was not the case. I learned this lesson the hard way and perhaps that it is why it sticks with me today. Everyone is hit with adversity; those who attack it conquer the challenges presented.

It is okay to feel down, to feel powerless, and be fearful. But use these feelings and emotions for what they are, the ability to recognize that you need to pay extra attention to the issue at hand. I'm not sure how I developed the ability to stay positive, but I do know that it is a cycle for me that repeats itself every time I am faced with a challenge. The cycle goes something like this:

Disbelief in the situation. When a problem or difficult situation presents itself, I always doubt it is that bad and don't necessarily believe it is real. This coping mechanism allows me not to be too shocked and make rash decisions. Most of the time, this phase lasts about a day or two.

Recognition that the situation is real. After I have thought about the situation, I begin to believe it is real and will definitely need my attention. This phase generally lasts a couple of hours and quickly leads to the next phase.

Fear and then anger. Once I realize that the situation is real, I feel both fear and anger at the same time. When I was younger this phase could last for a week, but over time it has decreased to the point that I usually can get through it in less than a day, although at times it resurfaces later.

Imagining possible solutions. The fear and anger stage leads to the most productive stage where I begin to imagine solutions and work through them in my mind. I've found that writing them down in a journal is helpful, because often the possibilities can be overwhelming and impossible to envision at the same time. This phase varies greatly for me, depending upon the complexity of the issue at hand. I've gone through this inner brainstorming session for weeks at times.

Trial and error. Probably the most engaging phase of my cycle, this is the time where I actually try to solve the problem and develop a concrete plan to move forward. When it works, it can go quickly, but most of the time, I make tweaks and in some cases, drastically change course. This method of real time learning, adjusting, and pushing forward develops the mind, builds muscle memory for the future, and is actually exhilarating. In this phase I find it is very easy to stay positive as I am fully engaged in problem solving, which I love.

Architecture school is a lesson in problem solving. I believe most designers are taught a wonderful problem-solving process. I am very grateful that I went to architecture school, which I credit to an unbending desire to solve the problem fully and completely. I'm not sure if this type of problem solving is taught in other disciplines but I do know that design thinking works. I find that when I am actively solving a problem, it helps me stay positive. I think it is important to move through the process as quickly as you can so that you can exude positivity to your organization as fast as possible.

Keep Those Around You Calm

One of a leader's most important jobs is to keep those around you calm, especially during difficult times. Use your experience to let them know that everything will be okay. But you can't just tell them; your actions and your demeanor will speak volumes. You need to show them that you believe things will be okay. That will help keep them calm.

When things were the toughest for us, and even now when we go through difficult times, John and I will first discuss outside the office, get our emotions in check, and then enter the office with a calming confidence. This is very difficult for me, as I am one of those people who wears his emotions on his sleeve, but over the years I have gotten better.

I remember once when I was a young architect, experiencing my first set of office layoffs, I was terrified. I watched as one by one those who sat around me were gone until there were only a few of us left at the office. I went in and spoke with my boss, whom I really admired. I asked what was going on and if he was worried. I'll never forget what he told me. "Craig, I may be a little worried on the inside, but not on the outside. I am confident enough to know this is just a phase and that soon we will be busy again." His calmness helped me and I offered to help. I doubled down on my efforts, as did he, and it wasn't long until the desks were filling up and again the firm was very busy.

That memory has stuck with me all these years. I can be a little worried on the inside but need to be calm on the outside. When we were in the midst of our financial crisis, I tried my best to model a cool calmness to the staff. I succeeded well enough to keep them from leaving our firm, working through the process, and eventually the tough times also passed.

Finding Your Rock

I wrote in a previous chapter about how important it is to have a confidant, a touchstone who will listen without prejudice. Finding this person is not always easy but is essential to being a good leader. Frequent talks with someone will help you stay positive and lead with a positive attitude. Positivity breeds positivity, just as negativity breeds negativity.

I have found that finding your rock does not always need to be a person. While I am not an overtly religious person, I am a person of faith. I believe in God and pray regularly. During this time, I began praying differently, however. I remember reading the book, *Blue Like Jazz*, many years ago. There is a construct in the book about praying for things; I think the author refers to this method of praying as viewing God as a slot machine. Prior to the difficult time, I think I always viewed God like that, praying for things that would make me happy and satisfied. My view changed significantly in 2011. I found myself praying for others, praying for strength, and praying for the courage to make life better for others. I found that it made me more satisfied with life and my ability to control the things within my control, and helped me stay more positive.

I adopted a practice of thinking of all the wonderful things that happen to me on a given day. I think about this as I go to bed which leads to me being thankful. I then pray for the good fortune of those who are connected to me, both family and friends.

I remember thinking that good leadership is not about being in charge, but taking care of those in your charge. Not sure who said that first, but they are words to live by.

Model Behavior

It is one thing to be positive; it is another thing to model positive behavior. Both are necessary characteristics of leadership. There is an old saying, "Don't just listen to what someone says, watch what they do." This is never truer than when you are a leader. Your actions speak way louder than your words, and when your behaviors and your language are not aligned, your credibility and ability to lead are undermined.

You cannot say you care about your clients and staff yet not return their calls or say good morning when you walk by someone. You cannot say you value honesty and then talk behind someone's back. Your behavior is magnified when you are viewed as the leader, and even the littlest disconnects between what you profess and how you act can become large issues.

Modeling behavior takes practice, but being in complete alignment will pay dividends in the long run.

Make Time for Yourself

During my time of crisis, I neglected many things in my life, most notably diet and exercise. I was completely consumed with working and worrying, leaving little time for myself. Even when exhausted, I stayed steadfast in putting in the extra time. While this may seem to be admirable, it led me down a very unhealthy path. I was overweight, out of shape, and my blood pressure had risen to the point that my doctor prescribed medication.

In February 2013 I attended a conference with my friend Mike McGettigan. Mike is a swimmer and in very good shape. I was complaining to him about my weight and he suggested that I go see his friend Paul Rosenberg who had just started a new gym. I called Paul and scheduled an appointment.

I've never been more intimidated in my life than the day I entered Real Results Fitness. Paul asked me to meet with him in a loft office, one I could barely fit in because of the spiral staircase. As I looked around, I saw very fit people doing exercises I had never seen before, led by strong and energetic trainers. The gym specialized in circuit training and overall fitness and nutrition.

Paul was gracious, however, and introduced me to two of the trainers who said that if I followed the plan, I could also become fit. I agreed to sign up for the 90-day program, ironically called the Real 90 program. The program had a nutrition component where participants logged in meals and brought their book each time they came to work out. For me, that was three times a week. The first week I could barely reach down to tie my shoes, let alone do some of the exercise movements. But week by week, month by month, the weight disappeared and I became more fit. After the first 90 days I was hooked and my workout sessions at the gym became more than just fitness. They became my escape from everything, my third place, my respite, and they were so helpful in improving my health.

I have been going continuously to Real Results Fitness ever since and although my needs have changed over the years because of recovering from injuries or surgeries, Real Results remains an important aspect of my life. My trainer, Mike Hayden, has become a good friend. He knows how to push me and also how to slow me down to keep me from hurting myself. Exercise and nutrition have become an integral part of my lifestyle, not just a fad or a diet.

It is important to make time for yourself. It could be doing anything that you desire—hiking, reading, creating art, or fitness. But do it. It cleanses the mind, strengthens the body, and has a great effect on one's soul. The me-time will also help you become a better leader.

Lead as a Marketer

Have you ever met a marketer who was not positive? I don't think it is in their nature. Marketers live in the possibilities, the potential, and the possible. I believe that the marketer mindset is essential in becoming a good leader. I'm not saying that all marketers should be leaders, but the DNA of a marketing professional lends itself well to true leadership.

There are three essential traits of marketers that are also essential to leadership: the ability to communicate effectively, the ability to see the big picture and the small details, and the enthusiastic ability to influence others.

Communicate effectively. Leadership requires the ability to be clear, concise, and steadfast in one's communications. Those who rely on you for decisions and direction need you to communicate consistently and be sure that the message is heard the way it was intended. This takes a bit of practice and a desire to make sure one is understood. Ask questions, ask people to paraphrase back to you what was just said. This simple practice will pay large dividends for you and it will help you know when you are communicating effectively.

Seeing the big picture and understanding the details. Most marketers have an uncanny knack of being able to hold two world views at the same time: being at the 50,000 foot level, and also seeing the details in the work. This ability to hold multiple views allows us to work better with our teams and help them see the sum of the parts and not just the parts. Those who can lead from within the work also have a leg up on those who cannot.

Ability to enthusiastically influence others. Influence is another important aspect of leadership. There are times when one must be able to help people see the direction that must be taken, prior to them seeing it for themselves. Marketers have an innate ability to make the case and rally people around an idea or a process. This is a very valuable attribute to leadership and cannot be understated.

Staying positive in the midst of both firm and personal adversity is very important for your leadership to gain traction. I promise you that the more positive you can remain, the better you prepare yourself for true leadership.

LESSON FIVE

PREPARING TO LEAD

LESSON FIVE

Preparing to Lead

Leadership is something not many consciously prepare themselves for. But since leadership is a process of learning, practicing, and learning again, it is critical to apply some rigor to the situation. The more prepared you can become in the aspects of leadership, the better you will be the day you are tasked in leading a project team, a group, a department, or a company. It is never too early to begin practicing and preparing for that eventual day.

A great way to prepare for leadership is to raise your hand. There are countless opportunities to practice leadership through volunteering for many community and professional organizations. This is a safe way to practice and you'll be doing something worthwhile at the same time. Volunteer at your church, your favorite nonprofit, or at your professional society. These groups are always looking for committee and board members where you will get great hands-on experience that cannot be replicated. Plus, you will be working with others where you have so many opportunities to learn. So put your hand in the air, find an organization you believe in, and volunteer.

Differences Between Management and Leadership

Before you set off on the path of learning how to lead, it is imperative you understand the difference between leadership and management.

We manage things, we lead people.

We manage projects, processes, tasks, events, and work flow. We lead people. Don't think you can manage a person; it is too unpredictable. You lead people by understanding who they are, what motivates them, what style of leadership they prefer, and how they listen and respond to situations.

Leadership is an art while management is more of a science with more predictability and cause-and-effect relationships.

Become Comfortable with Ambiguity

Contrary to popular belief, no one becomes a leader because they have all the answers. In fact, having all of the answers is not possible or when it is, it is not the type of decision that needs real leadership. When all of the information is available to make a decision, the decision is usually pretty easy. I equate the difference between leadership and management to the amount of information that is available. If everything is known, then you must manage the process. If information is missing, leadership bridges the gap to make sound decisions. Therefore, becoming comfortable when all of the information is not available is paramount to being a good leader.

The path to learning how to lead without all of the information is not an easy journey. It takes time because it relies upon your ability to develop confidence in yourself. Confidence comes with experience. I'm reminded of the old adage 'good decisions come from experience, and experience comes from making bad decisions.' So, yes, you will make some bad decisions along the way. The sooner you can develop a mindset that knows you can recover from a bad decision, the easier it will be to make decisions in a timely manner.

One way I like to work through a decision-making process when all the information is not known is to try and get to the root of the issue. Confronted with an issue, I ask why this is an issue. Then I ask why about my answer and then why again about this answer. I continue this process until I cannot answer anymore. I then analyze my answers and see if it helps me get to a truer decision. This process always works for me and helps me to sort through things.

Readers are Leaders

When I was young, I really hated to read. If only I would have developed a love for reading and learning when I was in high school and college, there is no telling how much easier learning leadership would've been for me. But I bumbled along, skimmed my reading assignments and guessed my way through academia.

The founding partner of our firm was an avid reader who shared many books with me. He was also really good at sharing relevant articles and book passages with the whole office in preparation of our staff meetings.

I'll never forget in one of the staff meetings, I declared that I had not read the material and questioned why we were doing this exercise. My partner did not say anything in the meeting and moved on to the topic of the day. On the drive home that night, I thought, *Why am I being so stupid? He's just trying to help me grow my capacity and I'm fighting him.*

The next day I came into the office and apologized to everyone for my stupid comments and began to develop a greater appreciation for the readings and the learning.

My partner told me that if I am to be taken seriously as a leader, I need to be well-versed in many topics and concepts. He was absolutely right. As I began to read, the world started opening up, which fueled my desire to read even more. The books flew by and I really started learning. I never learned as much so quickly as I did that year. The more I read the more I wanted to read. Reading opened up a whole new world for me and I credit that moment in the office meeting as being a significant catalyst in my development.

There are more books written on leadership than any other subject. If you search 'leadership' on amazon.com, over 60,000 titles are found. So, pick one, read it, and ask friends for recommendations. If one book isn't resonating with you, put it down, read another one and come back to it. Sometimes we need to learn something before we can appreciate another concept. But please develop a love for reading.

The more you read, the more prepared you will be to lead.

Explore

You cannot be a good leader just sitting behind your desk and communicating through email. Good leaders know the people they work with, communicate in person, and genuinely care for their well-being. You cannot do that chained to your desk. Get up, walk around, explore your office, and check in on people—their work, their growth, and their lives.

One process I developed during the stressful recession was to walk through the office at least a couple of times per day. I usually did this first thing when I arrived at the office. This allowed me to say good morning and check in with people prior to them being so engaged with work that I was an interruption. I also think the end of the day as people are packing up to leave is another good time. I've found these two daily check-ins have allowed me to have really good conversations with those I work with and at the same time, provided me with leadership opportunities. I've found that people will open up more toward the end of the day and that is an opportunity for deep conversation.

Know Yourself

To be an effective leader, you really need to know yourself—what makes you tick, what are your positive attributes, what are your negative attributes, and what lurks within your shadows. While this is easy to say, it is very difficult to do. You need to really analyze yourself and be able to see what is not on the surface. In his book, *Seat of the Soul*, Gary Zhukov writes about the need to authentically know who we are to be able to emerge as what we are meant to be. This book is required reading if you want to learn about yourself.

I found that journaling is an important aspect of understanding who you are. Write down the things you are dealing with on any given day, your reactions, and why you feel the way you do in different situations. Pay attention to your behaviors and your tendencies as that is where the real self emerges.

Lolly Daskal writes in her book, *The Leadership Gap*, about the things that get in the way of a person's greatness. I highly encourage you to read her book and to pay specific attention to the seven archetypes she identifies and their shadow sides. She identifies the following:

> The Rebel who is driven by confidence but becomes the Imposter, plagued by self doubt;

> The Explorer who's fueled by intuition, but becomes the Exploiter, a master of manipulation;

> The Truth Teller, who embraces candor, but becomes the Deceiver who creates suspicion;

> The Hero, who embodies courage, but becomes the Bystander, an outright coward at dealing with the issues;

> The Inventor, brimming with integrity, but becomes the morally corrupt Destroyer;

> The Navigator, who trusts and is trusted, but becomes the Fixer, endlessly arrogant;

> and;

> The Knight, for whom loyalty is everything, but becomes the Mercenary, completely self-serving;

These archetypes are explained clearly and elegantly in Ms. Daskal's book and need to be understood to help you grow in your leadership capacity. They form an important framework of integrity and the ability to recognize why and when you act on your shadow side. Recognition and understanding is first and foremost to changing behavior.

I see these shadows every day emerge within me. Sometimes I catch them and sometimes only when it is too late. But I realized a long time ago, knowing yourself and appreciating your gifts are a lifelong work in progress.

Don't Let Your Ego Get in the Way

Ego is a funny thing. Some say that to be successful, one must have a strong ego; others say that ego is always bad. My belief is that we all have one; it's how we choose to embrace it and what behaviors it causes in us that really matter. Ego can turn into great characteristics like confidence, belief in yourself, and knowing that things will turn out okay. Sometimes, however, ego can turn into stubbornness and inflexibility. That is true for me and it really gets in the way of making rational and good decisions.

Remember my partner I told you I fired in a previous chapter? Well, he didn't just disappear and go about his business. As much as I had hoped he would move on and find himself a new path, this did not happen. He felt wronged and pushed out of a company with nothing to show for it. Initially, he asked the firm for $25,000 to settle up and in exchange return his stock certificate. At the time, both John and I thought this was a ridiculous number and refused to pay. In our opinion, he violated our agreement and didn't deserve a dime. Our attorney agreed with us and we decided to ignore his requests. Oh, how hindsight is 20/20.

In early 2014, we were convinced by our attorney to sue our former partner to return the stock certificate. Our attorney's reasoning was that as the company recovered and began to clear the debt, we needed to protect ourselves from a lawsuit where the company was actually worth something. We agreed with him and moved forward. We should have seen what happened next, but our egos got in the way. We had poked the bear.

Our former partner lawyered up and counter-sued us, pushing the case into arbitration. There were several counter claims, including wrongful termination and a host of others. This was getting real. But our attorney continued to tell us not to worry, that the law was on our side and we were steadfast in our belief that we did nothing wrong.

The arbitration process lasted almost a year, between depositions, filings, etc. As we began to run up legal bills, we kept telling ourselves that we would win and the legal fees would be reimbursed. But what I never realized then was the cost of unproductive time. I was a mess going through the process. I couldn't focus on anything else. I lost all the momentum I had built up over the past two years and my stubbornness would not let me step back and rethink the whole process.

Over the year, we had two critical times when we could've settled the suit. The first for $35,000 and the second for $65,000. But we knew we would win and our egos got in the way. This was not about money to us, this was about principle, and we needed to teach him a lesson. That stubbornness cost us dearly.

The arbitration hearing took a full week of anguish. Sitting in the same room with my former partner was horrible and his attorney was as demeaning as possible. He was doing his job. After the week, eight of the nine claims were dismissed, but the arbitrator found that we should not have terminated our former partner without compensation for his stock. He was awarded $250,000. Add to that the $70,000 we paid in our legal fees was a devastating blow to the company.

We could've settled this issue for less than ten percent of this, but my stubbornness and ego got in the way.

Two important lessons I take forward from this are:

1. if you have a chance to settle a suit before it happens, give it considerable thought, even when you know you are right. Make the appropriate business decision; consider not only the cost of settlement, the cost of potentially losing, but also the stranded cost of non-productive time and diminishment of energy.
2. Never go to arbitration if you don't need to, especially if your company is seen as the larger party in the suit. Arbitration takes as much time as going to court, but the rules are way more lax and you could get stuck with an arbitrator who is sympathetic to the little guy.

But the real lesson lies in keeping your ego and stubbornness in check.

There are so many ways you can prepare yourself to lead. I've touched on many in this chapter, but my advice is that every time you have an opportunity to demonstrate leadership, every time you have an opportunity to make a decision in accordance with you values, do so. These small things will position you and create great habits. And these habits will help you to be ready when one day leadership chooses you.

EPILOGUE

As I complete this book, the world is recovering from the COVID-19 pandemic, a devastating time both personally and professionally. We will all clearly remember where we were in early March of 2020 when our worlds were turned upside down. That day, many of us become afraid of something we could not see and isolated ourselves into our homes to learn how remote work may be accomplished. Businesses were upended, projects and engagements were stopped as we watched our collective economies collapse.

But because of what I experienced from 2011—2015, I was no longer afraid of the pandemic's effect on our business. I was able to act decisively, clear and purposeful. I was able to mentor my younger partners in real time, and John and I knew that this would not bring us down. All the things we experienced together built a quiet confidence that things would work out if we stay focused on the tasks at hand. We did not let this uncertainty cloud us of the fact that we had a great business, great people, and great clients.

My experiences from the great recession and our self-inflicted reactions to it leave me with a sense of gratitude I never had previously. I am not afraid anymore. I am completely thankful for those around me, our clients, our friends, and most of all, my family.

Without the counsel and support of so many, I would not be the leader that I am. Even though I was reluctant to lead, I found out that I had the gifts to be able to do so and that the harder I worked, the more my gifts showed up.

I am comfortable knowing that I am continually growing and moving to become the leader I was meant to be and I am enjoying the journey.

I am no longer The Reluctant Leader.

BIO

A principal at LGA Architecture in Las Vegas, Craig Galati brings his passion for leadership to every engagement. He is an accomplished architect, consultant, and speaker who enjoys his time with family and friends. His most important accomplishments include being married to his wife, Sally, for 38 years, and their two sons, Corin and Carson.

Printed in the United States
by Baker & Taylor Publisher Services